Original title:
The Quest for Purpose, Interrupted by Naps

Copyright © 2025 Creative Arts Management OÜ
All rights reserved.

Author: Giselle Montgomery
ISBN HARDBACK: 978-1-80566-040-8
ISBN PAPERBACK: 978-1-80566-335-5

Halting Pursuits

Chasing dreams with napping shoes,
I stumbled hard, don't know the clues.
A pillow calls, my brain's at stake,
In a daze, a half-baked cake.

Plans are drawn in sleepy haze,
Yet all I see are blurry rays.
A coffee cup, now half asleep,
Minds at play, while bodies creep.

Slumbering Aspirations

Chasing stars with heavy lids,
Wanderlust turned into kids.
With every snooze, a map is lost,
In dreams, achieving at what cost?

In slapstick hopes, I take a dive,
But nap attacks keep dreams alive.
The world awaits, or so it seems,
But oh, sweet bed! You've stolen dreams.

Interrupted Journeys

On bikes and trains, the journey starts,
Yet zzz's hit like whirlpool darts.
With snacks in hand, the timer's set,
But snooze alarms are my duet.

A map in hand, but lost in thought,
Between adventures, dreams are sought.
The heart races but eyelids close,
Oh, the travails of a couch potato.

Respite Reveries

I dream of heights I want to scale,
But wake to see my hair a tale.
The couch, a friend, in secret guides,
Through daring sails and sleepy tides.

As visions fade to pastel hues,
In napland's grip, I find my muse.
Between ambition and soft embrace,
I laugh and nap in this odd space.

Interlude of Hope

In a world of dreams and schemes,
I found my path, or so it seems.
But just as I began to soar,
A pillow called, I hit the floor.

Snoozing through a grand design,
With open eyes, I sip my wine.
An epic tale, or maybe not,
A nap is worth a thousand thoughts.

I chased my goals with zest and zeal,
Until my blanket made its deal.
With snores that echo dreams untold,
Unraveled plans left in the cold.

Yet in each doze, a gleam of light,
Where visions dance, and ideas ignite.
So here's to dreams that come and go,
And naps that steal the fiery glow.

Moments in the Quiet

With every whim and fleeting thought,
I charted paths, just like I ought.
But alas, the siren song,
Of nap-time came, where I belong.

The clock ticks on, a race against time,
Yet here I lie, in perfect rhyme.
Plans swirling round, my mind's a mess,
But can't resist a cozy press.

Epiphanies may cross my mind,
But dreams are better when unconfined.
So let's embrace the idle spree,
As purpose rests, and sets us free.

Within the hush, there's laughter found,
As sleepy sighs and giggles sound.
With every nap, a wink to fate,
Who knew that dreams could just wait?

The Nap-Time Navigator

With dreams of far-off lands I soar,
But wait, the couch is calling, oh so more.
My heart's a compass, pointing to delight,
Yet eyelids droop, and I surrender to the night.

Beneath a blanket, I drift away,
My thoughts of gold maps begin to sway.
The treasure's hidden, but what's the clue?
Just five more minutes—and maybe two!

Rested Wakefulness' Embrace

Awake with vigor, a plan in mind,
Yet snooze buttons claim me, oh so kind.
Ambitions dance like butterflies in flight,
While I'm snuggled up, avoiding the light.

A world of dreams paints vibrant scenes,
But the pillow beckons—oh, what does it mean?
I promise to rise, tomorrow's the day,
Or at least, that's what I tell myself today!

Adventures of the Heavy Eyelids

With a backpack filled with hopes and schemes,
I set off for glory, or so it seems.
Yet a cozy cloud floats, soft as can be,
And suddenly the world's a sleepy sea.

Each journey starts with a grand parade,
But in naps, the finest plans do fade.
A treasure map sketched in slumber's embrace,
But waking me up? Now that's quite the chase!

Drifting towards Tomorrow

I chart my path with giggles and cheer,
But visions of snacks suddenly appear.
So off I wander, to munch and to snack,
And find a comfy spot to lay my pack.

As stars twinkle bright in the sleeping sky,
I reckon my plans will just have to fly.
With a belly full of dreams, I doze without care,
Tomorrow looks bright—if I get out of this chair!

Chasing Shadows

I ran to catch the fading light,
But tripped on dreams that took to flight.
Chasing shapes that danced and played,
I found a cozy spot to stay.

The finish line was miles away,
But my eyelids had a game to play.
With every blink, the world would shift,
Each snooze my mind began to gift.

Catching Z's

I plotted paths and grand designs,
But those soft sheets held better signs.
In the midst of a wild thought,
I drifted off—oh, what I caught!

Dreams of gold and silver spoons,
Turning wild ideas into tunes.
Yet in slumber's warm embrace,
I lost my drive, forgot the race.

Awakening to Potential

I woke with plans to change the world,
Yet my blanket was so tightly curled!
Pulled by goals, I started slow,
But back to dreamland I would go.

New ambitions like stars in space,
But the pillow's pull, I can't erase.
Awake, then sleep, it's all a blur,
Chasing dreams that never stir.

Fleeting Goals in Drowsy Gaze

With coffee brewed, I made my list,
But eyelids drooped, and I'd insist:
Just a quick rest, I'll be right back,
Till thoughts grew fuzzy, lost the track.

Goals like jelly, wobbled wide,
While comfy beds still beckoned, sighed.
Chasing dreams that twinkled bright,
While snoozing through the day and night.

Time Stopped for a Nap

The clock spins round, a hamster's wheel,
While I lie still, lost in reel.
A mission planned to seize the day,
Yet in my dreams, I float away.

Hours pass in soft embrace,
While visions dance in sleepy space.
The world waits as I take a break,
For dreams are where I choose to wake.

The Art of Lazy Exploration

With snacks in hand, we roam the day,
Adventure waits, but so does play.
A couch, a blanket, the ultimate lure,
Exploring dreams, of that we're sure.

Maps are spread, but so are crumbs,
Our mind's a wanderer, while the body slums.
A trip to the fridge, a journey supreme,
Each snack a treasure, a glutton's dream.

The Pause that Refreshes

With each grand plan, a nap crept in,
Mastering sleep with a cheeky grin.
Just five more minutes, the clock's my foe,
Each snooze a detour, that much I know.

Dreams may scatter like confetti bright,
While reality holds on, a little too tight.
Yet in those siestas, inspiration blooms,
Like flowers laughing in sunlit rooms.

Moments Flee, Slumber Calls

The world spins fast, yet I stay still,
Chasing half-dreams, my sleepy thrill.
Purpose hides beneath eyelids' close,
As forty winks carry me where it goes.

To find the meaning, oh what a race,
But the snooze button's hit without a trace.
A pirate of pillows, I wrestle with fate,
A sea of dreams, where I'm never late.

Doses of Inspiration

Plotting my path over coffee and toast,
But the warm embrace of dreams I love most.
Each yawn a siren, calling me near,
In the land of nod, thoughts crystal clear.

Awake again? Well, that's the plan,
But inspiration sleeps, in the arms of a fan.
A genius in slumber, I wake with a laugh,
Chasing my dreams down a comical path.

The Naptime Chronicles

In a world of dreams so bright,
I planned to soar, to reach new heights.
But eyelids dropped, the couch did call,
My purpose paused, I'd take the fall.

Maps and goals, so neatly laid,
Yet here I lie, a sleepy shade.
With pillow soft, my mind does drift,
Oh, mission lost, it's quite the gift!

Dreams of power, wealth, and fame,
Yet drifting off becomes the game.
Instead of wisdom, thoughts just flop,
As z's are counted, plans will drop.

A grand explorer in my dreams,
While snoring softly, so it seems.
I tackle giants and slay the beast,
Then wake to crumbs—a midnight feast!

Whispers of a Distant Dream

With a grand horizon up ahead,
I whip my plans, then rest my head.
A whisper calls—achieve, achieve!
But cozy beds make it hard to leave.

The stars align for bold pursuits,
Yet all I hear are napping hoots.
My dreams are rich with epic quests,
But snores emerge, ignoring tests.

The map is set, my heart is light,
But cozy blankets soothe my plight.
With visions hazy of what might be,
I close my eyes and count to three.

A hero's tale can wait, I guess,
As pillows cradle, sweet caress.
For fleeting moments, plans may pause,
In dreamland's bliss, there are no laws!

Stopping Midway

In pursuit of dreams, I sweep the floor,
But halfway there? I snooze, then snore.
An epic journey met with the yawn,
A grand adventure? It's just the dawn.

With boundless energy, I burst from bed,
But five more minutes race through my head.
To chase the stars, or clutch the sheets?
The choice is made—my mind retreats.

Plans scribbled down, so wildly drawn,
Yet sleep steals time, and where's the dawn?
I blink and dream, in a sleepy daze,
As purpose fades in the napping haze.

So here I lie, the world a blur,
While chores and thoughts can wait for sure.
With visions dancing, the clock hands creep,
In blissful silence, I'm lost in sleep!

Serene Disruptions

Pursuing life with zeal and zest,
Then sleep's embrace turns into rest.
A chipper smile becomes a frown,
For naps do sneak and take me down.

Plans of grandeur fill my head,
Yet there's a rest I'd much prefer instead.
With every mindless moment spent,
I doze off, free from management.

To chart my path, I seek the light,
But then the blanket wraps me tight.
Oh, sweet distraction, so serene,
With dreams of cakes and flying beans!

Ambitions rise, and gently fall,
As naptime claims my final call.
In this wild world of hopes and sighs,
I just might conquer—if I could rise!

When Dreams Collide with Reality

I thought I'd conquer mountains high,
But then I heard my pillow sigh.
Adventures fade, my plans await,
As snores begin to punctuate.

With visions grand of feats so bold,
I dripped into a nap so cold.
Where once was purpose, now just yawn,
With dreams of snacks till light of dawn.

Intermissions of the Soul

My spirit seeks a joyful chase,
Yet finds a blanket warm embrace.
Between the goals of daily grind,
I find my heart is quite maligned.

Each time I plan to save the day,
A cozy couch leads me astray.
I'll save the world when I wake up,
But for now, I'll just sip from my cup.

The Resting Road

I mapped out life, a vibrant thread,
Yet naps keep beckoning instead.
A detour here, a blink away,
My path transformed to a buffet.

Great adventures call my name,
But sleepy eyes just play their game.
With fuzzy thoughts and random snacks,
I'm led astray by cozy tracks.

Drowsy Epiphanies

Amidst the chaos of my mind,
A light bulb flickers, then unwinds.
As I decree my plans so grand,
I drift away, an idle hand.

A moment's pause for thoughts to bloom,
Transitioning to comfy gloom.
Realizations should take flight,
But only in my dreams at night.

Reveries of the Restless

In a world where dreams collide,
I chase my thoughts, they run and hide.
With coffee brewed, my mind's awake,
But one more snooze, oh, make no mistake!

Plans unfold like laundry tossed,
Yet in my plans, I find I'm lost.
A nap's a friend, a cozy steal,
As I forget my grand ideal!

Halfway Through the Awakening

I sit up straight, the clock's my foe,
But eyelids droop, oh, no, not so!
A quest for zest in the morning sun,
Yet slipping back, I'd rather have fun!

With socks mismatched, like life's own dance,
I take a step, then lose my chance.
The sofa calls, a siren's tune,
Just five more minutes, I'll rise by noon!

Paused Journeys

Adventure waits, the map's unfurled,
But where's the snack? Oh, my head's in a whirl.
I grab the gear, but trip on the rug,
A moment's pause, a cozy hug.

Off I go, but suddenly drawn,
To pillows soft, I serenely yawn.
Oh, quest for glory, can't you wait?
One more snooze, just let me be late!

Slumber's Whisper

The wildest dreams, they come and go,
Yet here I lie, caught in limbo.
A pirate's life or astronaut's flight,
But first, please let me snooze tonight!

While legends seek their shining prize,
I close my eyes, in snoozy guise.
Oh, laughter burst, for here I nap,
In sleepy state, I'll plan my map!

Dreams on Hold

In a world of plans so grand,
I laid my thoughts in the sand.
Each time I reached for the sky,
A cozy blanket caught my eye.

Chasing goals that slipped away,
Just as the sun began to sway.
With a yawn and a stretch so wide,
I drift into dreams, my dreams aside.

A to-do list that grew too tall,
Yet here I am with the cat and all.
As visions shrank in sleepy bliss,
I pondered what I might have missed.

So I rest my head, it's time to snooze,
With scattered thoughts and fleeting clues.
Tomorrow's hopes can take a seat,
For now, let the pillows feel my feet.

Siestas and Sentences

In the midst of wordy fights,
My eyelids pull down, oh what a sight!
The pages blur, the ink does sway,
As sleepy thoughts begin to play.

I draft a plan that sounds so bright,
But first I'll take a nap tonight.
With dreams of plans and schemes galore,
A cozy couch is hard to ignore.

I rise at three, with coffee in hand,
But my brilliant thoughts slip like sand.
They vanish quick, like morning dew,
As I contemplate the best snooze too.

So here I am, with goals amiss,
In my paper fort, I find my bliss.
While ambitions nap, I catch some Z's,
And wake to find no plans, just cheese!

Ambitions in a Sleepy Frame

I set my sights on the stars above,
But suddenly, I feel a shove.
The lure of pillows, soft and wide,
Calls to me from the other side.

With dreams of making grand escape,
I drift away in my sleepy cape.
My mission pauses, my goals on hold,
As I snuggle up and drift from bold.

Each nap a chapter, each sigh an arch,
In this unwritten tale, I'll march.
Yet every snooze steals time away,
As I wonder what I lost today.

Awakened by a snack or two,
Plans reboot—what am I to do?
With every yawn, ambition wanes,
But oh, the joy of pillow gains!

Whispers of Tomorrow

Dreams whisper softly 'Wake up soon',
But oh, this couch feels like a boon.
With every minute I briefly steal,
I ponder if ambition's real.

A list of tasks that grows each day,
But in this moment, I choose to play.
With a nap that stretches into night,
I find my peace — everything feels right.

I'll rise at dawn, or maybe noon,
And fabricate a brand new tune.
But first, again, I close my eyes,
And in my dreams, I wear the skies.

So here's to naps, the dreams that fade,
To the sidetracks, where joy is made.
Tomorrow waits, with arms so wide,
But for now, I'll let my dreams decide.

Sojourns in Stillness

In the midst of a fevered chase,
I found a bed, a cozy space.
Dreams danced gently on the sheets,
While my goals took a backseat.

Chasing schemes, I took a pause,
Yet snoring loudly, I caused a buzz.
Plans plotted with mighty zeal,
Were swept away in dream's surreal.

The ticking clock just laughed and grinned,
My ambitions loudly pinned.
"Rest now," it seemed to jeer and taunt,
As I snored on with dreams to flaunt.

But in the land of half-wake dreams,
My purpose burst at the seams.
With a pillow hug, I'll find my way,
At least until the break of day.

Moments of Clarity in Slumber

Thoughts crystallized in dozing light,
As I drifted in the night.
Plans once bright, now fuzzy haze,
Glowing softly like a gaze.

In snooze mode, ideas wear a crown,
While visions of snacks drag me down.
Yet clarity rarely shows its face,
When pillows hold me in their embrace.

I woke to find my notes were scribbles,
Like secrets told in silly giggles.
Yet laughter sprouts from dreams so odd,
In sleep, I'm both genius and god.

Awake again but dazed and slow,
Chasing dreams like melted snow.
With clarity noted in blurry quilt,
I'll rise again—perhaps with guilt.

The Art of Brief Respite

In pursuit of wisdom, I come to rest,
But who knew naps would be the best?
A quick retreat from worldly cares,
Turns into hours of silly dares.

The clock keeps ticking, but I'm not fussed,
In snuggly dreams, I feel I must.
Sprouting plans of grandeur and fame,
Only to wake with a comical shame.

Post-it notes with doodles galore,
Becomes treasure maps on my floor.
Adventure calls but sleep's in charge,
As I found a nap that's quite large.

So in this dance of z's and dreams,
Where laughter's stitched within the seams,
I'll slip away and take a chance,
For every dream deserves a dance.

Tracing the Lines of Intent

With a cup of coffee, I set my sights,
On chasing down deliberate delights.
Yet layers of sleep draw me near,
Where intentions blur and disappear.

I trace the lines of thoughts anew,
But snooze takes hold, it's true, it's true!
Mighty plans reduced to a nap,
My brain retreats like a cat in a lap.

Scripted dreams come forth at last,
As I futz and fumble under the cast.
Awake for moments, then back to snooze,
This endless cycle is a charming ruse.

So I'll sketch my hopes in fuzzy dreams,
Where silliness always reigns, it seems.
Intentions dance like butterflies,
In a slumber world where reason flies.

The Road to Comfort

I set forth on a path so wide,
With snacks packed tight, my trusty guide.
Yet every step, a sleepy sigh,
The cozy couch catches my eye.

I stroll through dreams, both bright and bold,
Every thought a story yet untold.
But just a wink, oh just a glance,
Turns my adventure into a trance.

With visions of treasures, I wander far,
Yet snooze on the map, how bizarre!
I chase the sun, a goofy race,
Then find myself in a napping space.

So here's my fate, with snacks in hand,
To nap in comfort, that's the plan!
The journey may pause, but hey, that's cool,
In dreamland, I'm nobody's fool!

Drift into Possibilities

I chase the clouds, a wild balloon,
While plotting my dreams from dusk till noon.
But eyelids droop, the world blurs bright,
And possibilities float out of sight.

With a blanket hug, I drift away,
To lands of ice cream and endless play.
The whims of thought, they start to dance,
Yet all I'm doing is taking a chance.

Oh, the fun I'd have if I just stayed awake,
But here comes the yawning, a big mistake!
I ponder greatness from my cozy nest,
While unreachable goals are put to rest.

So sit back world, I'll nap first, I swear,
When I wake up, who knows what I'll dare?
Until then, I'll let my mind roam free,
In my sleepy state, just me and Z!

The Silent Pursuit

In a world of hustle, I seek and strive,
My mind's a whirl, but it's hard to thrive.
As I wrangle dreams with purpose in sight,
A mattress calls, and oh, what delight!

Pursuing the great, or what I believe,
Yet every hour gets hard to conceive.
I plan and plot, then what? I collapse,
Into delicious, uninterrupted naps.

The chase is on, yet softly I slide,
Into slumber's arms, my nap-time guide.
What riches I seek fade into a blur,
As I cozy up, my thoughts all awhir.

So if you see me, don't give me a poke,
In dreams, I'm a king, in dreams, I invoke.
Tomorrow I'll rise, fierce and awake,
For now, just a snooze, for sweet victory's sake!

Z's of Creation

Imagination sparks like fireworks bright,
Yet eyelids droop, and dreams take flight.
From brainstorms of gold to snoozes of gray,
Creation can wait, I think I'll stay.

With every tick, the ideas swirl,
But oh that yawn; my vision's a whirl.
I pen down a thought, it starts to escape,
Plan of greatness, but take a nap? Yes, tape!

In my creative zone, a cozy retreat,
Masterpieces form but must stop for a seat.
Time for a snuggle, my mind's on the blink,
Who knew that dreams would make my heart sink?

So yes, the world's filled with wonders to seek,
And joyful pursuits that make life unique.
But first, I'll nap, and then I'll pretend,
That 'Z's of creation' will have no end!

Milkmaid's Dilemma

The milk was fresh, the sun was bright,
But oh, those sheep just took to flight.
With buckets full and dreams so grand,
She stumbled back, nap at hand.

Chasing cows creates a fuss,
But what's so wrong with just a plus?
A cozy nook, a blanket spread,
Her head did nod, adventures fled.

Floating on Pillows of Hope

On clouds of fluff, she drifted high,
With thoughts of cheese, and pie, oh my!
A wink of sleep, a snore, it's true,
Her dreams took flight, as dreams will do.

The world below, a busy hum,
While she made friends with every crumb.
Determined paths turned into fun,
For in her dreams, she'd always run.

Pathways to Rest

A road of flowers, wide and bright,
A thought to ponder? Or just a bite?
With every step, her eyelids droop,
And soon she's lost within the loop.

A squirrel approached, with nuts in hand,
"Wake up," it squeaked, but she had planned.
For life's a game of zest and naps,
And so, the world is full of gaps.

In the Land of Half-Dreams

In slumber's grasp, her worries fade,
Kings of cheese, in robes displayed.
"Just five more minutes," she insists with glee,
As tiny mice dance waltzes quite free.

So here she sprawls, with visions grand,
While magic whispers, a gentle hand.
The quest for fun takes silly turns,
And in her heart, the laughter burns.

Breaths Between Goals

I chase my dreams with fervent glee,
Yet find myself on the couch, carefree.
A sandwich here, a snack or two,
Am I still striving, or just passing through?

With every call of caffeine and cake,
I ponder choices, which way to take?
But eyelids heavy, I drift away,
To a land where I conquer, or so I say.

Chasing Shadows of Slumber

I planned a venture, a grand quest spree,
Yet napping calls like a warm, cozy sea.
Maps lie scattered, my plans in a heap,
But first, let me just take a short peep.

Adventures waited, oh so near,
But oh, the pillow whispers sweetly here.
Just five more minutes, I softly plead,
And off to dreamland, my mind will lead.

Distant Horizons

The horizon beckons with glimmers bright,
I leap with joy, ready for the flight.
Yet as I run, my energy fades,
And a comfortable chair calls, serenades.

With dreams of glory, I aim for the skies,
But a snooze on the couch is my greatest prize.
I'll conquer tomorrow, I promise it's true,
But for now, this cozy nap will do.

Tired Eyes

Adventure awaits, or so they say,
But first a nap will surely make my day.
My goals seem critical, yet so far away,
Tired eyes beg for just one more play.

With zealous intentions, I start to dream,
Only to wake with a will to scheme.
But as I stretch and blink in the light,
I realize my plans are a comical sight.

Unraveled Threads of Desire

I plot and plan, my heart set on fire,
But inspiration fades like a forgotten squire.
Threads of ambition soon fray and tussle,
As I cuddle in blankets, lost in the hustle.

The chase of my goals feels like a race,
Yet with each snooze, I lose the pace.
Ideas unravel like yarn dropped astray,
Where dreams are a nap away—what can I say?

Journey's Breath and Drowsy Thoughts

Chasing dreams with sleepy feet,
Coffee's brewed, can't find a seat.
Maps of dreams are drawn in haze,
Naps invade my careful ways.

Waking up, the journey stalled,
Pillow calls, my plans are mauled.
Adventure waits, but first the snooze,
In this game, I love to lose.

Worlds await, horizons bright,
But phantoms of a cozy night.
Each attempt to gear up fast,
Ends in laughter, snoozing past.

So off I drift, a sleepy crew,
Hoping dreams will lead me through.
Or will I nap beneath the trees,
And wake to find I've missed the breeze?

The Nature of Interruption

Plans were made, a map in hand,
Then came that snooze, not so well planned.
To the couch, I made my case,
The quest is on…but first, a space.

Dosing off, the world does fade,
The roadmap's lost, but naps are made.
An epic quest towards the couch,
But here I am, with dreams to vouch.

Alarm goes off, the quest resumes,
Only to find it's nap-time's bloom.
Defeated by blankets, soft and warm,
Where was I headed? Oh, what a charm!

One more snooze, it's barely noon,
I dream of forests, oceans, moon.
With every blink, adventure fades,
As I doze in sleep's cascades.

Slumber's Gentle Call

Awake I rise, or so I thought,
A siren's call, a blanket caught.
Dreams of kingdoms, knights, and quests,
But first, I think I'll take some rests.

Maps and charts, all out of sight,
For pillows hug me, oh so tight.
Worlds may wait, but naps are now,
Snoozing softly, time I vow.

Suddenly awake, my goals ask why,
As I munch on pastries, oh my!
Adventure's temping, yet here I stay,
With slumber's gentle call at play.

But still the dreams are calling me,
To find my sword, to sail the sea.
Yet here I think, what time is it?
As dreams and doughnuts do commit.

Sails of the Dreamy Spirit

Set the sails, time to explore,
But oh, the couch calls out for more.
Adventure whispers, "Come, set sail!"
Yet here I am, lost in soft veil.

Open seas, a ship awaits,
But snoozy pillows tempting fates.
With every yawn, horizons blur,
Oh, where's my map? A sleep I stir.

Captain of dreams, where do we go?
With every nod, the winds do blow.
But naps are sly, they take the helm,
As dreams lead off this cozy realm.

Sailing past clouds, I take a peek,
Then off I drift, it's nap-time, sneak!
The journey promised is on pause,
As I sail through my dreamland jaws.

Wanderlust and Winks

I dream of places far and wide,
With maps and snacks all piled inside.
But every time my eyelids drop,
Adventure waits, a little hop.

The mountains call, the oceans roar,
Yet here I am, snoozing on the floor.
A world awaits beyond my bed,
But who can resist a cozy spread?

Through jungles wild, I surely would roam,
But the bed feels more like my true home.
So, suitcase packed but dreams on pause,
I snuggle in, give in to the cause.

One day I'll wander, but not today,
The call of slumber leads me astray.
In dreams I travel, just not awake,
With giggles and snoozes, my quest I make.

Hibernation of Hopes

Once a dreamer with eyes aglow,
Adventures planned in a lively flow.
But winter's chill and blankets thick,
My hopes go dormant with a little flick.

I set my sights on distant peaks,
Yet all I find are sleepy streaks.
With visions bold of travel and glee,
I'm napping soundly, just let me be.

The stars can wait, the sun can too,
I'll chase my dreams when my nap is through.
For now, I'll rest, let passions freeze,
In this cozy nook, I find my ease.

Tomorrow's another day for cheer,
When I awaken, adventures near.
But until then, it's peace I seek,
Just a slight snooze — I won't be weak.

Pausing at the Crossroads

I reached a junction in the road,
While pondering paths I seek to load.
Left or right? My head feels light,
Maybe just a quick snooze tonight!

A compass spins, but my eyes too heavy,
Adventure calls but my heart's unsteady.
I could explore the world up high,
Or cozy nap till the sun floats by.

Directions blur in drowsy haze,
As I drift off into dreamy ways.
Map on my lap, I close my eyes,
Unfolding dreams beneath the skies.

With every wink, the world can wait,
I'll delay my journey, it feels just great.
So here I pause, with smiles and snores,
Finding joy in slumber's open doors.

The Countdown to Daydreams

The clock ticks down to dreamtime's launch,
As I plot journeys with every haunch.
Tick, tock, my eyelids flutter,
Is that a plane? No, it's my butter!

Plans of grandeur dance in my mind,
While my body seeks comfort, so kind.
Counting moments 'til I can nap,
With aspirations tucked in my lap.

Adventures planned for when I rise,
But snuggled here, I'm dreaming skies.
So let the countdown slowly creep,
As I gracefully slide into gentle sleep.

For every journey starts with a yawn,
And who can resist a switch to fawn?
Tomorrow awaits with glee and schemes,
But first, my friends, it's time for dreams.

Unfinished Destinies

Chasing dreams with sleepy eyes,
Plans on paper, yet I lie.
The world spins round, but I'm still here,
In soft blankets, winter cheer.

A coffee cup that's half-full still,
My schedule's packed, yet I'm too chill.
Mid-sentence thoughts drift like a breeze,
Oh look, a nap! Who needs degrees?

Adventures planned for every hour,
But slumber calls, I feel its power.
With every snore, my fate takes flight,
Only to crash by dusk's dim light.

Perhaps tomorrow holds a spark,
But for now, I find my arc.
With humor wrapped in every yawn,
Unfinished paths greet a new dawn.

Nap Breaks and Life's Curves

Life's a ride, bumpy and loud,
I brave each twist, I stand proud.
But then I find a cozy chair,
And slip away without a care.

Plans and meetings fade like dreams,
When a soft pillow calls, it seems.
Yet there's a rhythm in every doze,
A dance with plans that nobody knows.

The universe throws its silly curves,
While I'm in snooze, the world still swerves.
Awake to chaos, wondering why,
My to-do list has gone awry.

But laughter comes when I recount,
The beats of naps, the purpose count.
With giggles shared and tales untold,
In life's weird jig, I find pure gold.

Awakened by Daydreams

With a blink, another hour's lost,
In daydreams, I count the cost.
What was I doing? A fleeting thought,
Oh right! A nap, the best I got.

Making plans like painters stroke,
Yet naps arrive like cheeky folks.
They nudge me gently into bliss,
Claiming time I thought I'd miss.

So here I am, with thoughts astray,
Finding purpose in the play.
Life's a puzzle, pieces drift,
In catnaps, I find my gift.

Awake again, still feeling hazed,
But life's a laugh, I'm not afraid.
For in the dreams I've intertwined,
I find the joy I sought to find.

Interludes of Serenity

A sunny day, the world aglow,
Yet here I sit with nowhere to go.
Plans unravel like yarn in hand,
As I drift off to a quiet land.

But laughter lurks behind each yawn,
In my slumber, the day is drawn.
Whispers of purpose creep and swirl,
In naps, I dream of a mischievous world.

Time ticks on, but does it matter?
With giggles echoing, hearts grow fatter.
Each interruption, a joyful surprise,
Dreams weave magic before my eyes.

So here's to naps that fill the soul,
In fleeting moments, I find my role.
With humor leading the dance of dreams,
Life's simpler when nothing seems.

When Sleep Met Ambition

In the dawn's light, plans take flight,
An agenda made, it feels so right.
But soon the eyelids start to droop,
And ambition slips into a loop.

Coffee brews and dreams arise,
Yet on the couch, I find surprise.
With blanket hugs, I take a dive,
For snooze is where my hopes revive.

I wake to find it half past two,
The grand ideas were but a view.
The schedule waits, unkind and sly,
Yet who could say no to a nap's lullaby?

Plans are scribbled, notes a mess,
But each catnap feels like a success.
In dreams, I conquer all I see,
Who knew success came with such glee?

Twilight of Intent

Intentions bright like evening stars,
Tick-tock goes the clock, oh, how time jars.
I gather thoughts, plan my great quest,
    But couch calling, I can't protest.

The pillow whispers, 'Just one more snooze,'
    The world awaits, but I choose to snooze.
In twilight haze, resolutions fade,
While in dreamland, I joyfully wade.

With visions of grand plans in tow,
The snoring chorus starts to grow.
But visions slip like sands of time,
As Z's replace the mountain to climb.

Morning light may bring regret,
But cozy dreams—oh, what a bet!
I'll wake refreshed, or so I hope,
To rediscover that elusive scope.

A Journey with No End

Maps unfurl, with routes so bold,
Yet who needs plans when dreams unfold?
Adventure calls, but so does bed,
With thoughts of wandering in my head.

I lace my shoes, prepare to go,
But here's a thought: just one quick show!
A Netflix binge to set the mood,
At the end, I lose my interlude.

Tomorrow, surely, I'll start anew,
But here's the thing—what to pursue?
A journey waits, and so does my nap,
For visions dance in a cozy wrap.

Exploration calls from the great unknown,
But who can resist a cryptic tone?
In dreamscape's clutch, I find a way,
And so my journey can surely stay.

Dreams on Deferred Time

Tick tock, the clock is slow,
While dreams in the mind begin to grow.
Plans set forth, like stars aligned,
Then nap time shuffles all that's designed.

Under blankets, my brain can play,
With hopes that hide until the day.
Why rush the path, when snooze is near?
Lost in thought, there's no need to fear.

Yet in the haze, a glimpse might spark,
Of goals and triumphs hidden in the dark.
I stir awake, but time's a thief,
Dreams deferred bring such relief.

So here's to plans that flop and shift,
For napping's an art—a perfect gift.
I'll rise again with purpose to climb,
But first, a quick dip in dream's sweet rhyme.

Sighs Beneath the Stars

Under the blanket of night so vast,
I ponder life choices, futures cast.
But the whispers of dreams, oh so sweet,
Pull me away from my midnight seat.

While galaxies twinkle in a grand dance,
I trip on my thoughts, lost in a trance.
Each sigh is a star, bursting with glee,
Yet all I can think of is 'five more z's.'

With every decision, I take a long pause,
Perhaps I'll figure it out—oh, look, there's a flaw!
The universe chuckles at my sleepy plight,
As I trade grand plans for a nap tonight.

But in this soft hush, where day meets the dark,
Laughter erupts like a joyful spark.
For purpose found not in daily grind,
But in the sweet slumber—oh, never confined!

Wandering Beneath Closed Eyelids

With eyes gently shut, I roam through dreams,
Exploring odd realms, or so it seems.
An adventure awaits on my pillow so wide,
While plans take a nap, let the chaos collide.

In lands made of candy, I frolic and play,
But alas, my nap timer calls me to stay.
With each jump I take, a soft snooze enthralls,
As I ponder lost socks on celestial balls.

I drift past the clouds, where the funny guys dwell,
Who chuckle at purpose, like 'What the hell?'
With giggles and snorts, they shrug at my plight,
Then I roll over, embracing the night.

So here I will wander, where dreams intertwine,
Finding lost hopes like some vintage wine.
In the hush of the dark, with my eyes softly sealed,\nPurpose can wait while my laughter's revealed!

The Path Less Snoozed

Amidst the hustle, a road less traveled,
Lies a comfy couch, where all thoughts unraveled.
With cushions as pillows and blankets as dreams,
Who needs a grand journey bursting at the seams?

The signpost reads 'ambition,' oh, what a jest,
When all I can think of is the softest nest.
Meandering thoughts lead to a field of fluff,
Where finding my purpose can never be tough.

While others rush past with plans shining bright,
I roll my eyes back and say, 'Not tonight!'
For there in my cozy, my mind takes a snooze,
In the land of intentions, I've got nothing to lose.

So laugh with me now in this drowsy domain,
Where purpose is puzzling, yet joy is unchained.
With eyelids all heavy, I embrace this new creed,
Sometimes the path less snoozed is just what you need!

Driftwood of Intentions

On a river of thoughts, I bobble along,
With driftwood of intentions—what could go wrong?
I carve out my plans on the surface with glee,
But then it's nap time, oh sweet jubilee!

As the current takes me past dreams and past goals,
I tumble and giggle, letting go of control.
Each ripple a chuckle, a giggling plight,
Sailing on slumber, the world feels just right.

But when I awake, my ambitions adrift,
I ponder if nap time might be my best gift.
With purpose redefined, in a funny twist,
It's the times that I napped that I truly can't resist.

So join me, my friends, on this whimsical ride,
Where dreams fill the boat, and we joyfully glide.
For with every soft snooze, my heart does ignite,
And purpose, I find, is best caught in twilight!

Resting Between Stars

Beneath the sky, I lie in space,
Chasing dreams at a leisurely pace.
Cosmic thoughts twirl and drift,
But oh! That pillow, it's such a gift.

Astronauts nap on the moon's soft side,
While shooting stars joke, they take a ride.
Milky Way whispers, 'Stay awhile,'
As I snooze through the void, a galaxy smile.

Comets zoom past, their tails ablaze,
I chuckle in dreams, lost in a haze.
Maybe tomorrow I'll make my mark,
But for now, let the universe spark.

So here I float, in starry delight,
Dreaming big dreams on this cosmic night.
When morning comes, I'll leap and run,
But first, dear clouds, let's have some fun!

Pillow Dreams and Purpose Streams

In a world where goals race and speed,
I find comfort in soft, fluffy heed.
Dreaming of fortune while cozy and warm,
Oh pillow, sweet pillow, you're my calm charm.

Intentions set sail on purpose streams,
Yet here I linger, awash in my dreams.
Frogs wear crowns in a whimsical thought,
Was I heading somewhere? I forgot!

A nap is a treasure, a rare little find,
While work waits outside, I'm blissfully blind.
The clock may tick, but I turn it down,
Sleeping my way through this busy town.

So, chase me not with your to-do lists,
I'm dancing with uses of naps that persist.
With laughter and giggles, I drift through the day,
Till purpose returns, in its own silly way!

Napping on the Road of Ambition

Life is a highway, but I take the exit,
Just a quick snooze, it's time I must get.
Ambition whispers, 'Hurry and strive!'
But my bed calls louder—it's good to feel alive!

GPS spinning with plans on a loop,
I dream of my future while stuck in a scoop.
Backseat dreaming with pillows galore,
While my aspirations gather dust by the door.

Every mile traveled is met with a yawn,
Yet visions of riches dance on the lawn.
Oh, the best laid plans may come with a nap,
Who needs a map when I'm lost in my cap?

So let the world hustle and bustle around,
I'll rise like a phoenix from dreams I have found.
For every snooze taken ignites my delight,
As I snooze through my journey, my future is bright!

Epiphanies in Lullabies

Cradled by rhythms of whispers and sighs,
I find my bright answers in sweet lullabies.
When the world's expectations are loud and unclear,
I dream up solutions that leave me in cheer.

Soft melodies dance through my lazy brain,
Thoughts swirling like clouds when I'm lazy on grain.
'What's your life's purpose?' a friend snickers loud,
But snoring in rhythm, I'll make them all proud.

Revelations emerge as I drift with a grin,
Each nap is a secret, a treasure within.
While others are toiling and working so hard,
I'm inventing my genius with dreams in my yard.

So riddle me this, as I float on soft air,
Who needs inspiration when dreams lead me there?
In the cradle of silence, I'll find what I seek,
With a chuckle and nap, I embrace my unique!

The Balance of Sleep and Striving.

In the chase of dreams, I sprint,
But oh, that cozy bed makes me squint.
Fueled by caffeine, I dance and twirl,
Then snooze comes knocking, oh what a whirl!

With ambition high and eyelids low,
I dream of triumph, then hear snore's flow.
A notebook waits, ideas to jot,
But the pillow, alas, claims all I've got.

When inspiration strikes, I set off fast,
Yet my afternoon haul barely lasts.
A nap here, a snooze there, I try to fight,
But my brain retreats to the land of night.

So here I am, a mix of jest,
Chasing my goals, but longing for rest.
Life's a balancing act, quite absurd,
Between dreams of gold and sleepy blurred.

Dreams of Wanderlust

I dreamed of mountains, forests so wide,
But first... a nap, let this dream reside.
With backpack packed and snacks in tow,
I snooze and snore, watch the sunset glow.

The road ahead calls, adventures galore,
Yet sleep pulls me back, I can't ignore.
A quick catnap, just a minor pause,
In my slumber, future trips inspire applause.

Between the snoozes, I sketch my plans,
Of sailing away on sun-kissed sands.
Yet visions fade as I drift back to dream,
Oh, the traveler's plight—what a funny theme!

But when I awake, refreshed and spry,
I'll conquer the world! Well, as soon as I try.
For now, it's snacks and the couch's embrace,
Adventure will wait—it's my sleepy pace.

Slumbering Aspirations

In the realm of dreams, I plot and scheme,
Skyscrapers built, fueled by coffee cream.
But as I chart my bold ascent,
A nap interrupts, like an uninvited guest.

I flip through my plans, they spark delight,
Then lie back down to bask in the light.
Oh, greatness awaits! But so does rest,
Who knew dreaming big would come with a quest?

With every ambition, I rise like a lance,
But snoozing calls me to this sweet dance.
Chasing goals just needs some shut-eye,
As ambitions nap, to the clouds, I float high.

Though dreams may wander in slumber's embrace,
I'll wake up refreshed to recapture my space.
For in this lighthearted race, we find,
That purpose blends well with a snoozing mind.

In Search of Lost Ambitions

I once had dreams, they sparkled bright,
Until that couch said, 'Just sleep tonight.'
With aims high-flying like kites in the sky,
But beneath the blanket, ambitions lie.

With coffee in hand, I rise from the floor,
To find my lost dreams, oh what a chore!
But just as I start, the nap fairy sighs,
And down I go, much to my surprise.

I peek back out, with a hopeful grin,
Only to hear snoring rising within.
Ambitions, I call! Can you hear my scream?
But success takes breaks—it's all part of the dream!

As I scheme and snooze, in absurdity caught,
I find inspiration in naps that I've sought.
So here's to the dreams that yawn and retreat,
For in every slumber, we simply can't cheat.

Travels of the Weighted Eye

With a heavy heart, I roam the streets,
Chasing dreams on drowsy feet.
A coffee cup in hand, I stride,
But one quick nap, and I subside.

The world spins on, a blur of light,
But my eyelids drop; oh, what a sight!
I miss the train and trip on my shoe,
Excuse me, folks, I need a snooze.

Maps unfold like a cozy quilt,
But eyelids flutter; oh, the guilt!
I snooze beneath a shady tree,
Awake to find my guide missing me.

When dreams collide with sunny skies,
I ponder life while in disguise.
A weighted eye, my pausing friend,
In this journey, naps won't end.

Hibernation of the Heart

In winter's chill, my heart retreats,
Tucked in blankets, oh, what a feat!
I search for love, yet sleep ensues,
A fine romance: me, my snooze.

Warm cocoa dreams and dream-filled sighs,
With every nap, love softly dies.
Hearts may race but lips are tight,
As I drift off at twelve last night.

The clock ticks on, time keeps its pace,
But here I am, in my sleepy place.
Awake for dinner, then back to dream,
My heart hibernates, or so it seems.

A newfound love? Just let it wait,
I'm busy with naps, it's quite a fate.
For now, my heart's in dreamy bliss,
A snooze, it seems, I'll never miss.

Naptime Navigation

A compass spins, directions blur,
But oh! What's this? A soft purr.
My navigation's off the map,
I'll set my course for a cozy nap.

The stars above begin to twinkle,
But on my pillow, I start to crinkle.
I drift and dream of lands afar,
Yet here I am, a catnap star.

The GPS says to turn left quick,
But I recline and count to six.
Wake up confused, where's my spot?
I gave up wandering—oh, what a thought!

As lunchtime calls, I hear the sound,
Of fries and dreams that spun around.
Yet, here I lounge, in sleepy cheer,
Naptime navigation brings me near.

Sidetracked by Serenity

I plan a path, oh, such delight,
But peace finds me in broad daylight.
A hammock calls, it's time to sway,
As worries float and drift away.

With every sigh, the world does pause,
Why move at all? I can take a cause.
Serenity's pull is strong and bold,
Each boring errand left untold.

To-do lists flop, and naps take charge,
Plans erased—my dreams are large.
Existing here—no rush, it seems,
Happiness found in napping dreams.

So here's to those who drift and float,
In the waters of sleep, take a boat.
For what is life, if not to stray,
Sidetracked by peace, come what may.

Dreamscapes Between Reality

In search of meaning, the clock ticks slow,
With thoughts that wander, where do they go?
A nap sneaks in, like a cat on a chair,
Dreams dip and dive without a care.

Ideas float by on a fluffy white cloud,
As I doze off, I'm feeling quite proud.
But wait! What was that bright thought I had?
Oh well, a quick snooze, it can't be that bad.

Pursuing ambitions while asleep in a chair,
Mixing up visions, like a wild affair.
The purpose elusive, like socks that don't pair,
But laughter erupts when I wake with a glare.

Do bustling dreams offer answers anew?
Or does life find its path, despite what I do?
Awake, slightly dazed, I'm ready to roam,
With purpose just waiting to welcome me home.

The Calming of Thirsty Souls

A thirst for meaning in cups half-full,
Sipping on daydreams, oh what a pull!
But as the eyelids drop with a chuckle,
A journey begins in a cozy snuggle.

Inside the mind, a barista at play,
Brews steaming thoughts, both light and gay.
Yet suddenly, nap-time steals the show,
I wake to find hope's a little too low.

Is purpose just coffee, strong and bold?
Or is it tea-time stories, warm and old?
With every slumber, I drink and I feast,
On dreams that say, "Naptime, at least!"

So raise a glass to sleepy delight,
Where meanings bubble up, then take flight.
A sip of wisdom, then doze for a while,
Finding joy in the quest, with a smile.

Exploratory Slumber

Each dreamy detour whispers, "Rest awhile,"
On the map of thoughts, I trace a wild mile.
Exploring the lands where my mind softly drifts,
Suddenly, brilliance appears in small shifts.

Awake, I stumble on the lines I forgot,
Like a traveler searching for the right spot.
The more that I snooze, the more that I find,
New roads to adventure, sweet dreams intertwined.

In my sleepy roam, I chase shadows and light,
With a yawn and a stretch, I embrace the night.
Every nap brings forth a wise old sage,
Handing out secrets, like gifts from a page.

Balancing quest and dreams, what a feat!
Like a circus performer juggling on feet.
In playful slumber, the answers may lie,
With a wink and a nap, I can surely fly.

Between Intentions and Siestas

Intentions are lofty, they shine like the sun,
Yet eyelids flutter, and then I am done.
Caught in the limbo of plans unfulfilled,
A nap pulls me under, a soft slide to chill.

In the pause of ambition, I find some delight,
Wandering dreamscapes, both silly and bright.
Where purpose is tangled in laughter and grace,
And life takes a nap in a warm, fuzzy place.

What's meant to be done can wait for a while,
As slumber brings forth a teasing smile.
For amidst all the dozing, wisdom appears,
Napping my way through my giggles and tears.

Between dreams of glory and slothy embrace,
I find that my journey's a fun, silly race.
With a laugh on my lips, I drift off again,
Finding treasure in naps and the joy they contain.

www.ingramcontent.com/pod-product-compliance
Lightning Source LLC
Chambersburg PA
CBHW071846160426
43209CB00003B/437